Guess What

Published in the United States of America by
Cherry Lake Publishing
Ann Arbor, Michigan
www.cherrylakepublishing.com

Content Adviser: Susan Heinrichs Gray
Reading Adviser: Marla Conn, ReadAbility, Inc.
Book Design: Felicia Macheske

Photo Credits: © Anan Kaewkhammul/Shutterstock.com, cover; © Darrenp/v, 1; © Eric Isselée/Shutterstock.com, 3, 11, 21, back cover; Florence McGinn/Shutterstock.com, 4; © gracious_tiger/Shutterstock.com, 7; © Andrew Burgess/Shutterstock.com, 8; © Eric Gevaert/Shutterstock.com, 12; © Richard J Ashcroft/Shutterstock.com, 15; © Can Stock Photo Inc. / anankkml, 17; © Kitch Bain/Shutterstock.com, 18; © Andrey_Kuzmin/Shutterstock.com, back cover

Library of Congress Cataloging-in-Publication Data

Calhoun, Kelly, author.
 High-speed hoppers / Kelly Calhoun.
  pages cm. — (Guess what)
 Summary: "Young children are natural problem solvers and always looking for answers, especially when it involves animals. Guess What: High-Speed Hoppers: Kangaroo provides young curious readers with striking visual clues and simply written hints. Using the photos and text, readers rely on visual literacy skills, reading, and reasoning as they solve the animal mystery. Clearly written facts give readers a deeper understanding of how the animal lives. Additional text features, including a glossary and an index, help students locate information and learn new words"— Provided by publisher.
 Audience: Ages 5-8.
 Audience: K to grade 3.
 Includes index.
 ISBN 978-1-63362-622-5 (hardcover) — ISBN 978-1-63362-802-1 (pdf) — ISBN 978-1-63362-712-3 (pbk.) — ISBN 978-1-63362-892-2 (ebook)
 1. Kangaroos—Juvenile literature. I. Title.

QL737.M35C35 2016
599.2'22—dc23

2015003095

Cherry Lake Publishing would like to acknowledge the work of The Partnership for 21st Century Skills.
Please visit *www.p21.org* for more information.

Printed in the United States of America
Corporate Graphics Inc.

Table of Contents

I'm good at seeing things that move.

I like to rest in the shade.

ZZZZZZZZ

My body is covered with thick fur.

I have a
strong tail
I use for
balance.

I have
long ears
that I can
move around.

I have a good sense of smell.

I have strong legs. I love to hop!

Boing!

When I was a baby, I lived in a pouch.

Do you know what I am?

I'm a Kangaroo!

About Kangaroos

1. A group of kangaroos is called a mob.

2. Kangaroos eat only plants.

3. A kangaroo baby is called a joey.

4. Kangaroos use their strong tails for balance.

5. A kangaroo can only hop forwards, not backwards.

Glossary

balance (BAL-uhns) steadiness

pouch (powch) a pocket in the body of some animal mothers for carrying their young

sense (sens) one of the powers a living being uses to learn about its surroundings

Index